Voices of the Land

Edited by Jamie Crelly Purinton
Photographs by Charles Lindsay

Voices of the Land

Foreword by Michael Pollan

CHELSEA GREEN PUBLISHING COMPANY • WHITE RIVER JUNCTION, VERMONT

Contents

FOREWORD BY MICHAEL POLLAN   vii

ON BODY OF WATER #901   1
Le Anne Schreiber

THREE OR THIRTY ACRES   4
Don MacLean

RAMPS FROM A RUGGED PATCH   8
Bill Bensen

SOGGY GROUND   13
Jennifer Brady-Connor

HUNTING FOR MUSHROOMS   17
Robbie Butler

NEATNESS IS NOT A VIRTUE   20
Charles Canham

WORKING FIELDS   25
Barry Chase

BEYOND POSSESSION   26
Jens Braun

ONLY IN WHISPERS   33
Barbara A. Hermance

A FEW GOATS AND CHICKENS   36
Linda Anderson

FOR SALE   41
Eleanor Garretson

TO THE NORMANSKILL   43
David Yezzi

WHO LIVES WITH YOU?   44
Erik Kiviat

CATHEDRALS, BARNS & PONDS   49
Allan Shope

NO UFO   52
Chris Garrity

A BEND IN THE ROAD   55
Laura Hammond Toonkel

SPRING VISITORS   58
Fernando Nottebohm

A PLACE IN MIND   62
Peter Forbes

ABOUT OUR CONTRIBUTORS   65

PLATES AND PHOTOGRAPHER'S
NOTE   69

ACKNOWLEDGMENTS   70

Foreword by Michael Pollan

THINK OF THIS BOOK as the literary equivalent of a casserole, a gift of welcome from your new neighbors. I wish I had received something like it when I first bought a place in the country twenty years ago. At the time, I was coming from the city, and I was carrying the city person's usual preconceptions about the country. Though I didn't realize it at the time, those preconceptions were rooted more deeply in certain aesthetic ideas—in notions of the picturesque—than in any real sense of what makes this place the place it is—the people, the work they did and do, and the history of their relationship to the land. And it wasn't until I figured that out, in a long and occasionally embarrassing process, that I could really begin to weave my house and land into the larger tapestry of my town.

Because I was impatient (because I hadn't gotten my casserole!) I impulsively made some big changes that I came to regret, changes that now make me wince. I wanted a pond, so I dug one—in precisely the wrong spot. I took apart a stonewall *(cringe)* because I'd run out of flat rocks for the patio I was building. I cut down a fruit tree that was shading the area I'd picked out for my vegetable garden, before I realized what it was (an heirloom apple variety). Basically, I had a picture in my head of what my farmhouse in the country should look like, and I got right to work bending the landscape to my image of it.

How much better off I would have been had I waited a year to do anything, took some time first to observe the turn of the seasons, the shifting pattern of shade from the trees, the path that rainwater liked to take around my property on its way to the river. Had I spent some time with my neighbors, I would have known about the excellent hard cider the farmer who previously lived here used to make from the apple tree I'd chopped down, or why, though a dairyman, he'd never had a pond where you might think a pond should be.

(Great view from the house, but soil's too gravelly there to hold water.)

No book can substitute for those priceless conversations with your neighbors, but this one might convince you at least to have them before leveling that old shed or chopping down that seemingly out of place tree. Had I read something like *Voices of the Land* before I went at my land with chain saw and bulldozer, I'm sure I would have come at the project in a completely different spirit—in a spirit, that is, of respect for the people and plants and animals who really created this place I now am said to "own."

One of the best things about this book is that it's not primarily written by writers, but by people with a great many different kinds of relationships to the land—by farmers, naturalists, hunters, gatherers and gardeners. We writers tend to view nature somewhat passively and picturesquely, as something of a spectator sport, when what we really need now—as a culture, as property owners—are the voices of people more deeply engaged in the land, active participants in its on-going life. Here are a dozen or so of those voices.

And though they may not be talking about your acres exactly, I think you'll find that the slant they bring, the implicit questions they pose, will lead you to interrogate your own land and your dreams for it in a completely different way. They supply that necessary third dimension to our usual 2-D picture of "the country." That, finally, is the real gift you hold in your hands, since it is not until you begin to see that this land you fell in love with is so much more than your image of it that you can really begin to inhabit it—and add your chapter to its history. ∾

On body of water #901

Le Anne Schreiber, writer

PERHAPS LIKE MANY OF YOU, I came to be living where I do by a circuitous route, one that can be charted on several kinds of maps. The simplest is the road map which took me from my suburban hometown of Evanston, Illinois, through several large American cities, including Houston, San Francisco, Boston and New York, and then led me to rural Columbia County, New York, where I first rented a house in the hamlet of Glenco Mills, then bought and renovated another in the village of Ancram, and then finally built a home of my own design on the edge of a peaceful little lake in Copake called Snyder Pond. Its 26 acres are officially known to the New York State Division of Lakes as Body of Water #901. The journey took me 53 years, but when I arrived at Snyder Pond two years ago, I felt as if the road had delivered me to the exact spot on the map of the universe that had been plotted for me back where it all began—in that Chicago suburb built on the edge of a much larger and much more tumultuous body of water, Lake Michigan.

I am not a woman who believes in destiny, and in no other facet of my life have I ever even subjectively felt that I was doing exactly what I was meant to be doing. So, as you might imagine, I have puzzled quite a bit in these past couple years over what it is that makes me feel so at home and at peace on the edge of this pond. I have found not one answer, but many, far more than I can share with you in this letter, but I will try to single out one that suggests how many different roads can lead to one place.

For as far back as I can remember, my mind has been stocked with ideas, or concepts, some planted there by others, some freely chosen. And I don't know about you, but I feel ideas almost as palpably as one feels oppressive heat or a fresh breeze. There have been certain ideas that possessed immediate and lasting appeal for me from the first time I encountered them. Usually they were just as a word or phrase whose impli-cations I quickly intuited. Only later, if at all, would I learn how others understood the idea.

One of those concepts was "web of life." I don't remember when or how I first heard that phrase, but it was probably in early adolescence, and the very words, "web of life," seized my imagination as an alternative to another phrase, "the chain of being." I understood that concept all too well, thanks to the nuns who taught at St. Nicholas Grammar School in Evanston. I knew my place in the chain of being, and it was a lowly one, just one link above the animal kingdom, and several links below, in this order: my older brother, my parents and all other married adults, lay teachers, nuns, priests, bish-ops, archbishops, cardinals, the Pope, saints, the angels in their ranks (cherubim, seraphim and so on), archangels, and the Holy Trinity.

I didn't like my place in the chain, and I didn't like the whole idea of the chain, which made me feel shackled, and the only alternative I knew was being entirely cut loose and plunging straight to hell. So the first time I heard the phrase "web of life," I didn't need to know exactly what it meant to hear in its very syllables an alternative and a challenge to the grip of that chain. The image and idea of the web seemed to offer the possibility of repositioning myself and everybody else. The web was so much more flexible, the lines of influ-ence running back and forth every which way, and not just hurtling down the chain of command and landing on the lowest links with all that accumulated force of gravity.

The only downside to the web was that with all those lines of influence running every which way, it would be hard to know who was pulling my string. My place in the chain was a given, and the chain was always jerked from above. In the web, there was no easy way to chart my place or to figure out whose action was leading to what consequence. If the challenge of the chain was accepting my place in it, the challenge of the web was finding my place in it. It is, of course, a challenge I am still engaged in, and one that I have learned can never be fully met.

But here on Snyder Pond I come closer than I ever have to understanding the intricacy of the web's interlacings, and the force of my own impact, for better and worse. When you build upon land never built upon before, on the edge of a small pond enclosed by wooded hillside and marsh, in closer proximity to its flux and pulsation than anyone has ever lived—at least in recorded history—you would have to be blind not to know that you have entered its mix from literally the first footfall. With each depression of my boot, something is crushed and something else is given its chance, and although that is always the case, here I can see it with my own eyes.

On a larger scale, if I place a small floating dock in the water, I see how it slows the flow of a current, how different organisms start to cluster there, attracting different concentrations of fish, or insects, or plants. Or I see the water level rise, threatening to fill the pipes of rare pitcher plants growing in the marsh. I find its cause in a beaver dam constructed over a narrowing of the outlet stream, and I know the decision is mine, to let alone or meddle, deconstruct the dam and save the plants, let alone and see what replaces them.

Building is meddling. If I had been tempted to forget that, the New York Department of Environmental Conservation, its elaborate permit process, and books of regulations, were there to remind me. But, I took my cues directly from the land, in the hope that the shelter I built myself might come to feel as uniquely right as the peaceful pond that had drawn me there.

Architecturally, finding one's rightful place in the web is called site-specificity, and although there were no Ten Commandments to guide me, I found many answers simply by watching and waiting. The gradual steps of descent from forested ridge down the hillside to marsh and finally water basin became the model for a roofline. The undulation and curve of shoreline determined its footprint. The land's colors and materials, particularly its stone, became the color and material of my home; its orientation to light became mine. These first decisions, essentially aesthetic ones, were perhaps the easiest to make, because I drew from the land's most apparent quality, its beauty. Understanding how that beauty is the sum of many interactions, and how I have entered the mix, became and remains the ongoing effort.

I have long since learned that I cannot predict all the ripples of effect any act of mine may set into motion, but I am forced and privileged to observe the most visible of those effects. I can't know my exact place in the web, but I cannot help but see and feel that I am indeed in it. The force of the chain is utterly broken. The web has me fully in its grasp, which feels more like an embrace.

I have written here of seeing the impact of my every footfall, but of course the effects run back and forth, leaving me altered as I alter. That is another letter, a long one. And this route I have tried to trace for you is only one of many that converge on what, for me, feels like the right place at the right time. ❧

Three or thirty acres

Don MacLean, organic farmer and planning board chairperson

I WRITE THIS AS ONE WHO WEARS TWO HATS. First, I am a farmer who works the land, strives to preserve and improve its beauty and fertility, and contributes to the preservation of a farm five generations in my wife's family. I also serve on my town planning board, working with the imperfect, limited, and sometimes clumsy tools of zoning and subdivision regulations in an attempt to control development, "encourage agriculture," and preserve the "predominantly open and rural character" of our town. I hope that my writing this letter is not considered an act of hubris. My years of farming and serving my community have taught me some things that you might find helpful. Anything I ask of you I would do myself.

What I see as "landscape" is something more than the meaning in common usage. Farming has attached me to this landscape in a relationship as deep and abiding as marriage. Everywhere I see beauty; I also see lifetimes of work. The stone walls were built to clear land for cultivation, the islands of trees in our fields grew from land too stony to plow, the crops we plant form ever-changing patterns of line and color through the seasons, and second growth forests now cover the hill beyond the creek where the cattle grazed eighty years ago. We have shaped this landscape and it has shaped us. As we work to preserve its beauty, we must also preserve the uses that helped create it.

Although large-scale residential development and industrial mining projects periodically garner the scrutiny and vocal opposition of our community, I believe that the most potent agent of change is the quiet but steady piece-by-piece subdivision of land for home building. More and more of us want to live and build here and maintain the things that attract us to this place, the very things that our increased presence changes. How we subdivide land, where we site our homes and how we build these new homes are all critical decisions made by individuals that affect our entire community.

In my mind I can imagine two pieces of land of a size and type commonly broken from the larger landscape: a three-acre "minimum lot size" piece cut from the corner of an old family farm and a thirty acre field and woodlot—large enough for a country estate. Look at these two with me and see them through a farmer's eyes. One of these may be very much like the land you own.

If you have three acres with road frontage cut from a corner of the farm, you have a small lot with a hundred acre back yard. A few iron pins with orange tape at the corners of an invisible line mark off all that is yours. Like most people with three acres, you probably won't build a mansion. The driveway, septic and house takes up about one acre, leaving you with two to play with. Two acres is a lot of land. There is room here to raise food and meat for a family, to cut some of your own firewood, or maybe plant a grove of black walnut trees to pay major bills forty years from now—all kinds of possibilities. If you do something special with your land and work it in the smallest of ways, it will teach you, humble you and reward you.

And what of the hundred acres of your neighbor's farm that borders the back of your lot? It rolls gently down to the first fence line, then across the lower field where the heifers are and back up to the farmhouse and barns. Corn, pasture, and hay. The farmer has seen this view many times. He sees its beauty even after putting up hay in sweltering heat or chopping corn in cold weather or chasing stray heifers back to the low lot. When the light is like this in the afternoon even he stops and takes notice.

But the beauty comes at a price and if you are willing to pay the smallest part, your neighbor will do the rest. Not much is asked of you. Certainly the farmer is responsible for maintaining this view. It is the handiwork of an entire family working harder than you can imagine for wages you would

scoff at. And from you, all that is asked is tolerance, under-standing, and respect. Tolerate the smells, dust, and noise. Understand that the farmer's schedule is determined more by nature and less by the calendar. Respect that people are doing the hard work of maintaining the landscape you enjoy. They are all that stands between your new home and the potential of up to thirty others like it in your view. You will be rewarded by access to this land and the friendship of the people who work it.

If you have recently purchased thirty acres of prime farmland with a wooded hilltop, everything I have said for the three acres is as true for thirty. You are justifiably excited about the view from the hilltop, but look too at the view from the bottom. Look at how this open land rises slowly at first to the fence line and then swiftly up to the wood lot on top. The farmer put the fence there to separate the steeper rocky pasture from the deeper tillable land below. Even though the multi-flora rose and cedar are reclaiming the upper portion for forest, you can see that it was once pasture. From below you see what the people who work this landscape see.

And here I make my only request as a passer-by. Look closely at the sloped ridge of the hilltop with the crown of oaks. How much of your new home do you want to see up there? How little of the land can you use if you wind the long driveway up to the top? If you dream to build your home up there, I might agree that it is a better choice than using up this fine fertile farmland at the bottom. But maybe there is a place somewhere between the two. As a passer-by I am saddened year by year to watch the dark ridgelines in evening increasingly punctuated by hilltop structures. I ask that you design and build looking from the bottom of the hill up, and not just from the top of the hill down.

It is spectacular at the top, with a long open view over the valley to the mountains. There is something in our nature that makes us want to place our home on the top of the hill, even though in the building of that home much of what makes this location desirable is lost. Just remember that if you are determined to build here, you owe it to those of us who love the mountain views as much as you do, to create something low and discreet. After all, your new home will be the most prominent feature of our mountain views.

You are in a unique position with this much land. You might get your hands into it and make a small farm of your own. If you do, you will want the advice and knowledge of your farming neighbors and you will find them helpful and supportive if they see you doing the hard work. There are also other ways to work your land. Agriculture in our towns is more and more dependent on rented land. If you offer your land to a farmer, you might maintain your open fields, benefit a farmer, and gain a substantial tax break. In essence, though you own your thirty acres and lease twenty to a farmer, your relationship to the land and those who work it is much like our neighbor with the three-acre lot. Anything you can do to keep your land open, active and fertile helps connect it to the larger landscape it was and is part of.

Now, my other hat and some planning questions for us to consider. What is the future of our active and abandoned farmlands? Will the fields continue to be worked? Will they continue to be split into three or thirty acre lots? Will we cluster homes in order to keep the best land open? Are we willing to live closer to our neighbors in order to share the benefit of open land together? Are we willing to live with more rules and control of property rights in order to maintain an "open and rural character" in our town? In my years of serving on the town planning board one facet of human behavior has become very clear. We hold property rights as sacred in our country and culture. But we maintain contradictory positions by both wanting the right to do what we want with our own land and wanting stricter controls on the use of all other land, especially our neighbors'. We can't have it both ways. If all the rules and regulations were in place to forever protect the view from your new home, you probably would not be allowed to build your home in the first place. We can have controls on property rights and development only to the extent that we can agree to certain standards as a community.

As a farmer, I urge you to work with and learn from your land. As a planning board member, I ask you to do two simple things. First, as you subdivide your land or build your home, act according to the rules you would write for your neighborhood. Second, get involved in your community, be it a town committee, fire department or neighborhood group. The interaction of working people, working land and volunteer service forms the very fabric of our rural community. It is why we are here. ❧

Ramps from a rugged patch

Bill Bensen, chef

IN DEFIANCE OF BUD-BREAK, snow clods cling spitefully to the north face of a stacked fieldstone wall. A harlequin wedge of Canadian geese wheels over the stubble of a parched cornfield. It's early spring in the Helderbergs. The first ramps pierce the sodden detritus of last year's bloom. Under a shifting cobweb of naked twigs I climb Hickory Hill to dig ramps in the sugar bush and feel always an overwhelming sense of smallness. With feet tenuously planted on a steep grade, I struggle to pry muddied roots from a stony slope, and wonder how many generations have done the same, how many more might enjoy the privilege.

A continent away, the feds are preparing to hack logging roads through the Tongas National Forest, one of the few pristine expanses of temperate rain forest left on the planet. How long before this old sugar bush suffers a similar fate, clear-cut to afford someone a better view of the Catskills to the south? Kneeling in the damp silence of the forest, happily untangling clusters of ramps, I needn't dwell on that prospect, but it's there, looming darkly. I think instead of the all-ramp dinner I will create from the wild larder of the forest: farm-raised chicken stuffed with lemon and ramps; hand-stretched strudel dough stuffed with roasted ramp bulbs, sheep's milk cheese and field greens. Expectant diners gather on a chilly spring evening, and the kitchen is perfumed with the scent of these muscular cousins of the cultivated leek.

Struggling back up the hill, under laden baskets yoked by a shovel, my thoughts return to those who came before me, and I marvel at the resilience of those who broke farmland out of such unyielding ground. They were tenant farmers, indentured to their hardscrabble homesteads, in the last days of the patroons. But with a tenacity, rooted in the promise of ownership, they endured, leaving behind a multi-generational legacy of good stewardship of the land.

Today most of the farms are gone. Vertically integrated agricultural conglomerates and the demand for cheap milk combined to force upon the family farmer a price structure that could not support the costs of 4:00 A.M. milkings and a life measured out by the hundredweight. The pastures that once provided a livelihood now yield up only "view sheds" and tax bills. And that legacy of good stewardship can profit its heirs only through subdivision and sale. Their experience should inform our own existence, telling us finally that no matter how long we remain upon the land, we are all only guests here.

"Here" is a rugged patch of forest in the southwest corner of Albany County, nearly dead center of the great basin that empties into the Hudson. A thousand of the same freshets I splash through while out ramping drain these hills and entwine to charge that river. Hericlitus said that one cannot step into the same river twice; it is a thing, paradoxically, both constant and transitory. So is the land. It is constant in its solidity, transitory in geological processes evolving over eons. In such a temporal context, our existence is a nanosecond. Yet what kind of guests we are during our brief stay matters greatly. The first settlers here learned that lesson when they stripped the forests of hemlock and destroyed the tanning industry they had created.

That is part of the reason I admire farmers; their livelihood is deeply connected to how well they care for the land. Also, as a chef and independent business owner, I feel a strong affinity with others in businesses that are capital and labor intensive, and that exist at the whim of the public and the capricious trends of popular culture. Over the years I have sought out local farmers, and have built a reputation on their products: organic mesclun greens, tiny fingerling potatoes, heirloom tomatoes, cheese pumpkins, pasture-raised turkey

and fresh goat's milk ricotta have all found a place on my restaurant tables. Despite a grassroots movement to support family farms, each year there seem to be fewer of them.

Several years ago, in another attempt to help support a local agriculture, I gathered together some farmers to start a weekly market outside my restaurant. The scale of it was as small as our village, but the products diverse and of high quality. We were unsure how people would respond.

Now, for twenty weeks each growing season customers gather, early on Saturday morning, like a hungry brood; they visit their favorite vendors for local maple syrup, fresh organic greens or French bread still wearing a glow from the oven. A children's group started a latte and lemonade stand across the street, donating the proceeds to local arts and conservation organizations. Something marvelous has happened. For a few hours each week a community find its center. Neighbors visit, connections are made, friendships form.

I ask myself how such a thing could happen so quickly, and the only answer is that it all rises from the land. It is that deeply atavistic connection we have to the earth; that which makes us stop at a roadside stand on our way home from a weekend in the country and buy far more apples than we will ever use.

Pericles of Athens said, "All things great of this earth flow into the city, because of the city's greatness." But when that greatness overwhelms its inhabitants, it is here that they come to escape. From here come great things of this earth that stock the greenmarkets of that city. It is here that the flow begins. ❧

Soggy ground

Jennifer Brady-Connor, biologist

ALTHOUGH SOGGY AND STRANGE, forbidding and buggy, the wetland behind my home is part of an intricate landscape. The cooler waters harbor northern two-lined salamanders among the golden saxifrage. The club-like masses of cattail flowers are home to moth larvae and other insects sought by chickadees. Dead trees jutting from the wet earth teem with chipmunks, squirrels, birds, and others that inhabit or forage in the crumbling wood. Even the malodorous skunk cabbage provides sanctuary for many small amphibians and insects.

Water flowing through continues along a journey that may be centuries old; the energy of this flow has reduced mountains to hills and has changed the courses of rivers and deltas. Spring floods, the ebb and flow of tides, droughts, and animal activities reclaim floodplains, deposit soil or debris, or dry and flood the same area repeatedly. From our wetland, the water will evaporate, replenish our atmosphere, sustain plants, shade and cool the earth, and flow on its journey from stream to ocean. Some of the water settles down and keeps the earth moist during the dry weather of summer, flowing again with the cool rains of fall and spring.

When water's journey is interrupted, it can impact the lifestyle and pocketbook of people living downstream. This idea became quite real to me when I headed back to my childhood home near the Tomhannock Reservoir in Pittstown, New York. My Dad still lives next to the town garages and the wetlands of Otter Creek. Most of the year parts of our backyard were quite squishy; kids heading toward the creek would laugh as they jumped across the wet parts, sometimes getting an ankle wet if they miscalculated. In the winter, water settled and froze into a smooth sheet used for ice-skating; in the summer, the ground grew the thickest, greenest grass in town. Every year the backyard flooded when the creek rose, combining with spring rain running off the still frozen ground. The

unexpected came one spring during a particularly drenching rainstorm. This time the flood of water came over the parking lots and paved yard of the town garages and flowed along our foundation, eroding the earth around it. When it was over, the ground in our earthen basement had caved, leaving the propane tank hanging precariously on the edge of a crevasse.

Apparently as the town grew, so did the fill and pavement. The town had slowly filled in wetlands for parking and storage and converted more and more upland to pavement and buildings. The water's journey shifted from flowing slowly across the land and into the wetlands to flowing quickly and in larger volumes across the pavement and building foundations towards the lowest place—our backyard.

Many years have passed and I now own a home. We have come to know and appreciate many of our wild neighbors. A box turtle, about 15 years old, visits almost yearly from the forest that adjoins our lands. She hefts herself along the terrain until she finds a location that, for some reason unknown to me, gets just enough protection and sunlight for her babies. We have come across a red fox with kits, foraging turkeys, nesting broad-winged hawks, and numerous red back, spotted and northern two-lined salamanders. Each spring a chorus of wood and green frogs and peepers serenade us nightly. These are but a few of the wild neighbors who share the land.

My husband and I have continued some simple activities over the years to maintain the character of the wetland and help reduce our impact on the watershed. We compost yard wastes in a contained area and use this rich material in our garden. We planted native rhododendrons and wildflowers to serve as a buffer that slows the flow of water, reduces soil erosion, and eliminates the need for pesticides. The new shed went into an area already significantly altered—our lawn. Pumping out the septic tank every couple of years helps keep organic contaminants from entering the landscape. By doing these little things we hope to help keep the water a little cleaner and keep our wild friends around.

A drop of water that lands on my rooftop follows a tremendous journey. It rolls down onto the ground, through the backyard and into the wetland. There it mingles with cool spring water and flows into a small unnamed brook where it continues on to Cold Creek. Cold Creek absorbs this raindrop, carrying it on to Fish Creek, where it once again joins a much larger body of water until it empties into the great Hudson River. Imagine, billions of billions of these raindrops, flowing down through the entire Hudson Valley, to make their way to the Atlantic Ocean. When each person gives thought to designing and building homes in harmony with the landscape, we enable these drops of water to remain clean and true to their journey. ❧

Hunting for mushrooms

Robbie Butler, silversmith

I HOPE YOU ENJOY THE BAG OF WILD GOODIES I have left at your door. Although we haven't met yet, I just wanted to introduce myself. I am a neighbor of yours. I am the guy who would rather pick mushrooms than shave. Let me start again, as that did not come out quite right. I want to congratulate you on buying a great piece of property. I realize that you do not need me or any of your neighbors telling you this and that about it; however, there is one thing I hope you will let me show you and, yes, it does have to do with shaving.

If it has rained all night long and it is any time between April and October, I set my alarm and go on a walk across the fields and into the woods at first light. Over the years, your property has become one of my favorite places to go as, with a little luck, I might stumble on a great find of any number of wild mushrooms. By the time I get back home, there usually is just enough time to throw a few of these mushrooms into a frying pan with a couple of eggs and get a thumbs up or down from my family before rushing to work. This is a typical spring or fall morning for us. So as you see, our friends are used to my irregular facial shadow. They also are used to brown bags of various fungi regularly showing up on their doorsteps.

You might be asking yourself who is this trespasser? And why does he choose to risk his and his family's life with wild mushrooms for breakfast, as well as look badly while doing it? Let me explain. Firstly, I do not "trespass" only on your land. No, all my neighbors are treated equally in this regard! To be fair, I am not really "trespassing" as I have permission to be walking their land, just the way they have permission to be walking my land. If, however, they were unavailable before the rains, or the hour was a little too early to call, then the aforementioned bag of thanks seems to do the trick.

Secondly, it is true that the wrong and sometimes quite beautiful common fungus can kill and can kill in a very pro-tracted and painful manner. This is worth the repetition because it is something that should be taken very seriously. My solution to this problem is to be boringly cautious and to stick to what I call the "idiot mushrooms." These are the mushrooms that once identified, preferably with an expert as your guide, you can pick year after year with the assurance that they have no poisonous look-alikes and never deviate from the expected.

So now I come to the part of this letter that I most want to write. Not being a writer, how do I tell you about the treasure that your land holds? Oh, don't take my word for it. Go see for yourself. Go for a walk after it has rained for three days and you need boots just to get across the field. Better yet, don't wait until the rain has stopped.

If it is late April, the first morning when the temperature is above 60 degrees, the morning misty, the smells loamy and heavy with life, and the sun growing brighter than anything you have seen for months, all will be gentle, wet and green. By a spot near the road, under a dead tree, you might just find a flush of a dozen or so cone shaped and pockmarked morels hiding in the grass. Some might be small and some might be as big as your hand.

In July, during the first rain of the month, walk up to the high oak forest. A fawn might startle you. Hawks may call and you will have to push through the summer flowers on the way to the cool of the woods. Once in the moss and leaf litter of the forest, along with 100 to 200-year-old oaks, a world of quiet cool light challenges you to find Black Trumpets or Horn of Plenty, a Chanterelle cousin that has a soft, mousy black calf-skin of apricot-smelling, edible joy.

Early in September, if you have been away and you're not sure if anything came out during the last rain, walk up the front of the gravelly hill to the small overgrown orchard on top. As you come down from the crest, you will find yourself in a birch forest. Try breaking off a twig from a black birch and taste its sweetness as you climb on the almost bare gravel, with ferns and moss as the only undergrowth. The wintergreen taste of the birch accents the whole experience of following deer paths in gravel left by glaciers. How could a fungus be happy here? After your eyes adjust to the light on the fallen yellow birch leaves, you will suddenly realize that a lot of mushrooms are very, very happy here. Though hard to see camouflaged in the leaves, these mushrooms grow out of a virtual underground "tree" of mycelium, the fungus body that the mushroom fruits from every year given enough rain. Mushrooms, in a funny way, are like apples growing on a tree with their millions of seed-like spore.

With only one small bag, you pull out your shirttail and fill it too with *Buletus edulis,* more commonly known as Cepes or Porcini, the favorite from Moscow to Rome. You have picked for an hour up and down the west side of the hill, leaving plenty behind. As you round the hill's north side, the habitat changes and not a mushroom is in sight.

In late October, it is getting cold. It may feel like snow tonight. This is the best time of all to be out because soon only skis will let you break into what will become winter's outdoor desert. The light is low and you don't have much time. In fact, you want to check on many of the oldest trees, not just any old tree but the great oaks. There are five, two on hedgerows and three in the forest.

One of the great oaks grows along the wall that runs through the wood. Another is on a steep, rocky stream bed. You draw near to the stately oak with a great huge torso of gray crowned with brown leaves that has proudly marked this wall for 250 years. It shows immediately what you have come for. Equally magnificent and weighing 20 to 30 pounds, the *Grifola frondosa* or Hen of the Woods sits at the foot of her benefactor with her back against the giant, her feet sunk in the rich humus at its base. This time you came prepared with an Adirondack basket. With a gentle tug and shake, in she goes. On to the next tree that lords over a steep rocky ledge above the small kill running down the hill with mushrooms growing on the north, south, east and west sides of the trunk. Only one, however, can fit in the basket on top of the first, so the others will be left to feed squirrels and creepies. Now, in the lowering light, only pride makes you finish the loop to see the other hens that you may—or may not—come back for.

So, this is what I, your neighbor, wanted you to see, hear, smell, touch and taste. All this bounty makes up just a few of the edible mushrooms, a few edible ones out of the thousands that one cannot eat. For many, those too become a world of wonder too numerous to begin to catalog. Their beauty and their variety are wonderful to behold even though they are not made to harvest. Really, it is less about picking mushrooms than about seeing and feeling the woods. Sure, my friends like the odd, wild delectable. And I like that they think I am clever and brave when really picking mushrooms is the easiest thing in the world to do carefully. All that is required is to just put on your boots and go to work unshaved once in awhile.

As for the goodies in the bag, just cook them with a little butter until tender. They are a gift from the great oaks. Enjoy. ❧

Neatness is not a virtue

Charles Canham, forest ecologist

I FELL IN LOVE WITH THE FORESTS OF THE HUDSON VALLEY as a teenager. Several of my teachers were persuaded that I could accomplish more out of school than in study hall. They let me take long lunch breaks and wander through the woods near my high school armed with a field guide to tree identification and a copy of Ewell Gibbons's book *Stalking the Wild Asparagus*. It was, after all, lunch time. At first, the forests appeared primeval and wild—a place where a natural order governed as a welcome contrast to the social chaos of the 1960s. It was impossible to walk far in those forests, however, without acknowledging the impact of humans. My most vivid memories of those walks are of finding mature trees growing out of the foundations of long-abandoned farmhouses. At first, I took this to be a graphic demonstration of the resilience of nature. Here were forests reclaiming land that early settlers had labored for many years to clear, plant, graze, and eventually abandon in favor of more fertile land in the Midwest.

Years later, I now know that roughly half of the forests of the Hudson Valley followed this path of forest clearing, intensive agriculture, abandonment, and reforestation. The other half of our current forestland was never cleared completely, but was used intensively for grazing, firewood and timber. Rather than a testament to the resilience of nature, I now see the land-use history of the Hudson Valley as a profound statement of the power of humans to transform landscapes, both deliberately and inadvertently. We clear-cut virtually all of the forests of the Catskills in the mid-1800s to use the bark to tan leather—in many cases leaving the logs to decay. We cleared three-quarters of the land in the valleys for farming, but began leaving as topsoil eroded, agricultural pests proliferated, yields declined, and the Erie Canal opened, providing a route west. The first European settlers in the town of Clinton, where I live in Dutchess County, didn't arrive

until roughly 1750. The town's population grew rapidly over the next seventy years, but then began a steady decline as farms were abandoned. The town's peak population from the early 1800s was not exceeded again until after World War II, when residential development of abandoned farms presaged the pattern of suburban development that is the dominant transformation in today's landscape.

The forests that reclaimed the land are beautiful, diverse, and productive. They are not, however, the same forests that were here before European settlers arrived. While trees have rapidly reclaimed former agricultural lands, the wildflowers that once grew here have been much slower to regain ground. Many of those wildflower species have very limited means of movement, and depend on agents such as gravity and ants to move their seeds. Some scientists suggest that it could take hundreds or even thousands of years for these species to re-establish themselves on former farmlands. The species of trees are quite different, as well. The first land surveyors in Dutchess County, who worked in the early 1700s, marked the corners of lots by recording the species and sizes of the nearest trees. These "witness tree" records provide a detailed picture of the pre-settlement forests. They document a landscape of unbroken forest, dominated by a number of different species of oak trees.

In the forests of current day Dutchess County, the oaks have yielded half of their dominance to both red and sugar maples. There is still debate among ecologists over the reasons for this change, but the most likely explanation is that suppression of wildfires during the past century has allowed the maples—which are very sensitive to fire—to take hold and displace the oaks, which possess a thick bark that protects them from the effects of ground fires. Finally, many of our native tree species have declined due to inadvertently introduced insects and diseases. The litany is long—chestnut

blight, Dutch elm disease, beech bark disease, dogwood anthracnose, and most recently, the hemlock wooly adelgid. As the native species decline, exotic species spread from our roadsides and gardens and take hold in our forests.

As land development pressures begin to reverse the tide of forest re-growth in our region, conservation organizations have focused on protecting the best and most diverse natural areas that are left. But it has become clear that private land-owners hold the real key to the future of Hudson Valley forests. My own property includes a small bit of forest. The part of me that first took me into the forest as a teenager, and which still holds sway when I work in forests of more remote regions of the world, would love to stand back and watch nature take its course. All that I have learned since then, as a forest ecologist and scientist, tells me that this is not possible. With the power to so pervasively transform nature comes a responsibility to accept stewardship, particularly of the land I own. I am not separate from the ecology of my small wood-lot—I am part and parcel of it. In many ways, I am its key player.

I may be a key player, but I don't get to make the rules. That prerogative remains with nature. I share with many of my human neighbors a desire for neatness and aesthetics that is not shared by the other species that live in my woodlot. Ice storms and even freak October snowstorms have wreaked havoc on the trees on my property in recent decades. It takes real control to resist the urge to get out my chainsaw, my favorite landscaping tool, and clean up the debris.

Unfortunately, the "debris" is actually habitat for many species, and contains critical nutrients that need to be left in place to replenish the soil. Neatness is not a virtue in nature—in this my teenaged children appear to be closer to nature than I am. The leaves that fall to the ground each autumn carry essential nutrients back to the soil. Removing them for

even just several years in a row could be enough to create nutrient deficiencies in the soil. The resulting stress on trees may make them more vulnerable to insect pests and disease. Leaves and woody debris also provide critical habitat for many species of invertebrates, including rare native woodland snails. Many of those species are in turn fed on by other species, such as red-backed salamanders. Over the past decade, ecologists have discovered that the abundance of woody debris is the most critical, defining feature of the few remaining old growth forests in New England, and that the distinctive richness of species in those forests is due to the specialized habitat created by the standing snags and fallen, rotting logs of very large, dead trees.

Ecology is a science of messy detail, partly because evolution has provided such an extravagant diversity of species and interactions. But when you come right down to it, the starting point for good stewardship of the forests of the Hudson Valley is pretty simple, and mostly involves resisting the urge to do too much with too heavy a hand: don't clean up after nature unless it's necessary for safety; don't introduce new species unless you are sure they won't become invasive and spread out of control; don't fragment an intact forest into smaller pieces. Doctors are guided by the principle of "doing no harm." I suspect that this is also the first principle of good land stewardship. If this is true, then the most important prerequisite for good stewardship is to understand the ecological consequences of your actions.

While "doing no harm" may be the starting point for good stewardship, the pace and scope of human impact on the environment has reached a point where passive stewardship may no longer be sufficient. In the absence of active intervention, the pace of invasion of native forests by exotic species can only accelerate. While we often look to government agencies for solutions to environmental problem, it has become clear that the real power to control invasive species lies in the hands of committed landowners. As our forests have re-grown over the past 100 years, they have become an increasingly valuable economic asset. Logging has re-emerged as a common practice in Hudson Valley forests, albeit with much less public visibility than in previous centuries.

Unfortunately, much of the logging consists of "high-grading," in which the highest value trees are removed with little consideration to long-term economic or ecological consequences. Again, we often look to local governments to regulate logging, but it has become clear that enlightened landowners, rather than regulations, are the key to good forestry.

As you learn to listen to the land, with a little luck you can go beyond avoiding harm and begin to work with nature, rather than against it. Part of me would still like to believe that I can simply stand back and watch nature take its course. All that I have learned in twenty-five years of studying north-eastern forests tells me that this is no longer possible. ❧

Working fields

Barry Chase, dairy farmer

I AM A SECOND-GENERATION DAIRY FARMER whose passion for breeding a better dairy cow has kept me tied to the land for thirty years. We raise 125 head of registered Holstein cattle on 466 acres. We crop 225 of those acres in hay, corn and oats providing all the feed the animals require minus the soybean meal, which we purchase commercially. I am luckier than most because I'm doing what I love to do. There is great satisfaction in working with land and animals.

It's a shame everyone can't know the beauty and satisfaction of turning the earth each spring, seeing the plow glide through the ripe soil, turning furrow upon furrow, and creating a smooth dark carpet in its wake. The smell of newly mown alfalfa hay as it cures in summer is sweeter than tobacco. The pre-dawn day is serene, windless, and starlit. Each season's progression from planting through harvest and each successful step ensures the farm's survival for another year: oats planted in early April, a full hay mow by August, two silos topped off with corn silage by mid-October, and a crib bursting with ear corn before heavy snowfall.

My close relationship with the land makes it difficult for me to witness the changes that have been happening in our area over the last few years. As land changes hands, new owners tend to make dramatic changes, building new barns, buildings and driveways without a feel for the land or its ability to be productive. We are watching two major changes in our landscape. First, the best agricultural land is rented to crop farmers and the secondary and more marginal land is left to grow up to scrub brush and multiflora rose. This provides great cover for wild animals and birds, but before long becomes difficult to return to farming again. Second, horse farms are replacing the dairy farm. The land goes from being worked to being manicured. The farmhouse is restored and painted; new board fences bound the property. Everything is made beautiful, but this land will no longer experience crop rotation or be productive except to provide pasture and exercise for a few horses. Their feed will be purchased from somewhere else and the cycle of local production will come to an end.

Change is inevitable and an ideal scenario would include adequate and fair zoning regulations, which protect our neighbors and our community and allow for growth. I feel strongly that a landowner has every right to do as he wishes within existing zoning laws. I am not comfortable telling anyone how to live their life or spend their money. When all our neighbors were farmers we had less conflict. However, when conflict arose, our property rights within the law were not questioned. My new neighbors should receive the same standards.

There are no simple solutions. When you are accustomed to the open landscape, a new house is an eyesore, a new driveway a liability, and lights and noises an irritation. If we are lucky, the new landowners will not build the "pimple" on the hill or light their property with 24-hour security lights.

I continue to farm as the landscape changes around us. My cows offer their gifts of calves and milk, the land its harvest of hay and corn. Our farm cycle recurs daily and yearly. As you become my neighbor, I hope our common attachment to this land can bring us together. Our stories and our gifts can be the seeds sown to form our new community. ❧

Beyond possession

Jens Braun, Quaker and builder

THE OTHER DAY I RECEIVED a notice in the mail. A local lumberman had driven by our land, looked up the dimensions and boundaries of our 135-acre parcel at town hall, and sent us an offer to cut some of our trees. We would split the profit of the lumber sales. This is pretty straightforward and when done with the help of a good forester can be a good source of income and contribute to the long-term health of the woodlands.

I grew up in Ecuador. During high school I did as much mountain climbing as I could. One of my lasting memories is standing on the high peaks of the eastern cordillera and looking out across the South American continent towards Brazil and the Atlantic Ocean. I remember the low silver cloud cover, thousands of feet below me, spreading to the curve of the earth. Sometimes it would be instead the dark green of the Amazon rain forest, but it always spread, unbroken, as far as could be seen. From the tops of the mountains, I reveled in the view of the forests, knowing that the green I saw, or knew to exist under the cloud covers, was an uncountable number of trees, each different from the ones I knew, but each a wonder in its own way. Understanding this and knowing that one could hike to the edge of human influence on the planet, affected me deeply.

Starting from a young age, the jungle's trees took on meaning for me. These trees carried life in abundance. They had vines that grew up to their tops where they mingled with the orchids and other epiphytes. They were loud with the cries of parrots and sometimes monkeys. But most of all they were enormous. I was a good tree climber, but I never got up to the canopy on any tree; the trunk was too big to grasp, or there were too many thorns, or the moss was too slippery, or the vine's hold was too far out from the trunk, or most often, my arms or my nerve would begin to give out while I was only half-way up.

Although the land belongs to Ecuador and Brazil and parcels are registered in the name of small farmers, oil companies, Indian tribes, and others, I could imagine nobody really owned it. How could anyone claim to own such vastness, such wonderful diversity? Nobody fully grasps what is there. A person could say they owned it, but anything they did with this "property" would be a reduction or destruction of that which already existed. How can someone own the magnificence and life-carrying capacity of a mahogany giant that started growing before his or her great-grandparents were born? That mahogany could be converted to money, but the magnificence cannot, and when the tree becomes lumber, the magnificence is lost to the world. And, no matter what a person does, he or she will die, while the land will still be there and new things will grow and live. I have long carried in my psyche a resulting doubt about the concept and validity of land ownership.

This land on which I now live and which a lumberman can identify as my "property" in the town records, is about half fields and half forest. It was an abandoned farm when we bought it; several of the fields are giving way to aspen, birch, or pine saplings. The pond is nearly silted in and mostly marshy. Although I have rebuilt one of the two dilapidated structures on the land, I have essentially done little to the overgrown wild fields or woods in the time we have been here. I have spent much time walking the land, and know that foxes, coyotes, rabbits, a porcupine, a fisher, and bears walk here too. There are two, sometimes four, red-tailed hawks that soar the length and breadth of the acreage. A kestrel perches on the electric lines and in the treetops down by the swampy pond. Many other bird species spend time here, from perennial robins, to bluebirds and orioles, turkeys, waxwings and wood ducks. I know where grouse have nested and hatched their young. The amphibians speak out every evening from

early spring through the summer. Also in abundance are moths, spiders, crickets, wasps, butterflies, and other insects. I have gone out nights to look at stars and hardly lifted my vision skywards because of the firmament of fireflies across the still, open fields.

Also on my rambles, I have noticed where past human residents of this land have walked driven, or ridden. Once, in the middle of a dense section of the woods I noticed a leveling and followed a forgotten farm road around the steep knoll to the land's west side. The level route makes a wonderful cross-country ski path. There are places where one can find large, flat slabs of shale. I have used some of these, as have former residents, for steps into the house and a bridge over the seasonal creek leading to the pond. My daughter is a born flower arranger. She has helped me become familiar with the wild blooms of the warmer seasons, where they grow, and where they don't. The wildflowers tell us that the upper field was probably always pasture, for it is too rocky and too poor to have been planted with corn or other field crops.

And then there are trees to which I return time after time, including huge old hickories and enormous maples and oaks. I visit about a dozen feral apple trees that still produce tasty little apples in the fall. There are a couple of tall and rough cherries and many straight and lofty pines, as well as hemlocks that grow in magical spots. One of the old oaks split years ago when it was already massive. The fallen section is mostly returned to soil, but the standing part has healed, spread out over its decomposing half, and grown yet larger. These trees are not the complex ecosystems of the rainforest giants, yet they are wonderful in their own shapely beauty. Their changes through the seasons contrast with the seeming constancy of the never resting trees of the jungle. Both have in common that quality, so foreign to most of the animal kingdom, of time measured long.

In Ecuador, I thought of the sizes of trees, but did not focus on the passage of time. There the seasons do not leave growth rings and a tree matures in much the surroundings it experienced as a sapling. Here and now in the temperate zone, I look at the old trees and think about the winters they have known, the leaves they have dropped, and the farmers they have shaded. I consider the view in terms of time seen by the great red oak whose branches reach over the rock wall of the upper meadow.

Such trees, like those in the rainforest, refuse to be owned, despite my thoughts about milling some of them. I'd like to use them to build a home I could grow old in, set on a special warm and sheltered hillside of this land. Down by the stream there is a whole grove of oaks. This grove of tall, unbending trees could supply beams for a barn, to replace the one we are told burned down in the early 1980s. I consider whether the pride, utility, beauty, and income of a timber-framed barn could make up for the lost majesty of stumps. The cut trees would change shape but remain integral to this piece of land.

I know that according to one world view, I own this land and can perfectly well use it largely as I please. The imposing memory of another world view however, has a grip on me. I am coming to accept that I will change this land, and already have. But my shoulders aren't heavy about it because I know I have given the land a chance to change me too, and it already has. It seems odd, but in some way we have conversed. I talk about my plans for a barn or a home tucked into the south-facing hill, or the orchard and garden, while it talks about which tree to leave untouched and which field the fox kits use as a playground. Our recent conversation has been about the NO TRESPASSING signs posted around the boundaries. We both want the fisher and the bear to trespass. But what about trespassing people? The signs were placed by

former owners to keep other deer hunters off their private preserve and to let others know the location of property boundaries, and to protect the land for specific uses. I tell the land I want to do the same. Last fall I walked the boundaries to repost the signs. In my mind I ignored the words "Private Property" written black on orange and told the land that "No Trespassing" really means, "Don't cross the boundary that allows you to think of this place as merely a possession." The land and I have agreed that we may use some of the trees for shelter and other needs, maybe even to pay the taxes demanded by the other world view. But they will be carefully chosen and carefully cut.

Our upper meadow and woods are visible from many of the surrounding hills and roads. I am asked why I don't consider building my house up on the meadow where the views are most fantastic and expansive. Yes, but they are more so when I hike up there and look out while still conscious of the freshness of the air because I am breathing hard. My sons have camped up there to watch the sunrise. We celebrated my daughter's coming of age from that spot. I don't know why, but to build a house on that site, with its small fire circle, would diminish their memories of growing up. I see it in their eyes when the suggestion is made. Power lines and a driveway with five culverts could be built up to the high meadow, but would it be worth what is lost? It gives me pleasure to look over at the skyline of that meadow and woods from miles away. I want to look at a house up there as little as I wish to see the patterns of humanity when looking east from the top of Mount Cayambe. I am relieved that in my family's time here, that particular view is unlikely to change. ∞

Only in whispers

Barbara A. Hermance, realtor

YEARS AFTER THEIR PURCHASE, I hear my former customers talk about their properties with either words of endless delight or nagging dissatisfaction. The delighted ones most often started small, letting their knowledge of time, seasons, weather and land character alter their plans. Without exception, the dissatisfied regret moving too fast and doing too much. They brought civilization with them only to be disappointed by its impact, discovering too late that a man on a bulldozer is not a surgeon.

Some of the most wonderful real-estate success stories begin with a special piece of land and a simple house. On a pragmatic level, home resale often depends on determined factors of first impression such as unique locations, privacy, access to water, and views. Views are always in demand for resale, but thoughtful planning is necessary to make them work. I attended an open house several years ago at a spectacular hilltop home with 360-degree views. There was considerable comment among the brokers that despite the cost-no-object amenities of the home and the extraordinary view, it was just too windy to comfortably sit anywhere outside, even though it was a relatively calm day. Despite a half-mile of separation from the county road, traffic noise rolled over the open field and into the terraces and house.

On the opposite scale of the pristine and the unique, I have seen many parcels of land, at substantially below-market values, overlooked by buyers because they are in various stages of neglect. Young unregulated second growth, thick undergrowth, partially improved, or recently timbered, these parcels have lost much of their appeal. Here requires a different process of visualizing changes in terms of reclaiming and accentuating the positive. One of my clients has spent many hours in a labor of love to free a nineteenth century orchard from its hundred-year-old over-story forest. Another has gradually cleared the brush in an overgrown field to discover a once dry pond refilled and vibrant with wildlife again. Another was delighted to find that a tangle of grapevines, willow and alder hid an ancient spring complete with rock-lined grotto. They have all told me that it is a continuous adventure to uncover their surprises.

Some twenty-three years ago I had the great fortune to acquire a large parcel of land with my vintage home. Bounded on two sides by an enormous wetland, the land is a mixture of old fields, orchard, woodland, ponds and streams. The parcel has changed over time, matured, as I have changed my thoughts about what it is and what it should or should not become. There are countless hours of meandering walks behind me. Each has subtly or radically altered my thinking with new discoveries, sometimes in places I have passed before but never really seen. Perhaps the greatest gift has been learning how to listen—not hear, but listen.

On occasion, I have house guests with young children and for them the land is an irresistible lure. Together we take "adventures" on the condition that they may not speak unless they get my attention with hand contact and then only in whispers. It has been fascinating to watch the children, as the vehicle of language is denied, in an environment where fifty feet into the trees civilization ceases to exist. Senses on high alert, they are sponges for every experience. "Did you know, Mom, that swamps grow lilies taller than you? We saw cabbages with skunks in them and a huge blue bird that fishes with his nose and eats frogs!" Ninety minutes of impressions with senses magnified dominate the evening's conversations. Somehow, we never mind the endless repetitions because, tired as they are, the children crash like kittens, leaving all of the adults lighter of spirit in the afterglow of magic seen through their eyes. They have told me years later, as adults, that what they learned that day was how much they would have missed listening only to the sound of their own voices.

I have pondered on that and come to the conclusion that the lack of resources to carry out my civilizing plans for the land in the early years has reaped many rewards. I know better now from my business experience that the common desire to civilize with lawns, terraces, gardens, clearings, and buildings can inexorably erode the very thing that was most attractive about the land in the first place. I now wander my land in endless delight, understanding that the land has come to own me. I have become its guardian, rewarded as the ever-enchanted child. ๛

A few goats and chickens

Linda Anderson, broadcast journalist

I LIVE WHERE I WANT TO LIVE FOR THE REST OF MY LIFE. My home is in a beautiful pastoral place rich with diversity. In front of my house is a maple tree where a pair of wood ducks returns to nest every spring. Downy white feathers cascade from a hole in the tree and sometimes I find fragments of their eggshells on the ground. On walks I watch deer grazing in open fields. I have seen mink, beaver, fox, opossum, rabbits, raccoons, skunks, squirrels, coyotes, and once a moose. But the most wonderful and amazing thing about where I live is that it's in the heart of a small village called Cambridge, a place the author Tracy Kidder might describe as "a place where a person might live a whole life and consider it complete."

I can walk to everything I need, from a martini to a woodland trail. Here is a hospital, a library, post office, school, a coffee shop, bookstore, grocery store, restaurant, diner, and a theater. Our village has three streams with good fishing, wooded hillsides and open fields, all within its 1000 acres. Although I have a car, I use it as little as possible, for I have discovered the immeasurable pleasures of walking through our small town.

I didn't always live in the village. My husband and I once raised organic crops on a small farm, cultivating the land with the aid of a draft horse. But then I had a car accident, life changed, and we decided to give up the farm and move into the village. We had two school-age children at the time and figured village life would mean, rightly so, less driving. Our kids, now teenagers, walk to school, friends' houses, the grocery store, the diner, and jobs. This town gives them exercise and independence.

Village life is often overlooked. Most people seek property with oodles of acres that they hope will provide them with quiet and splendid views. Maybe so, but I think that peace and tranquility is more vulnerable "out there" than it is in the village. Someone who buys 40 acres is more likely to see changes in the landscape than those who live within the village. The homes in my neighborhood have stood here since the late 1800s, and are likely to stay. But while the structure of the village remains virtually the same, the fabric has changed.

Recently my village has been "discovered." It is currently experiencing probably the most profound changes since Native Americans were chased out around 1781. Houses that used to sit on the market forever are immediately snatched up. And as real estate prices rise so do tensions between the "locals" and the "newcomers." It's all such a delicate balance. At its best, this mix of new blood makes for a diverse and interesting community. At its worst, it creates arguments and misunderstandings.

My village continues to be a farming community. Over several decades it has managed to retain much of its rural and historic character. The out-buildings attest to this history. Behind almost every home is a carriage barn or chicken coop. If you have a minimum of five acres of land in the village, you may keep farm animals, and several families do. But now this old tradition is under attack.

Recent newcomers are feuding with neighbors over a few goats and chickens. "We did not move into a village to live next door to a farm," they say. But this is a rural county and a rural community. And the fact is, they moved into a village that allows farm animals. To complain about farming here is like moving to Manhattan and complaining about traffic noise and subway smells. Even without farms in the village, we would not be immune to the sounds and odors of the agriculture that surrounds us. In spring, farmers spread on their fields manure smelt for miles. From summer to fall tractors haul trailers loaded with corn or alfalfa through the village. Farming comes with the territory.

It would be one thing if the argument was confined to

the dispute between neighbors, but it has snowballed into a campaign to abolish all village farms. The consequence of that change would be devastating on many levels.

First of all, it threatens the preservation of open space in the village. We currently have a lovely ring of agricultural land along the village border that acts as a buffer—a gentle segue from the surrounding farmland into the village proper.

Eliminating village farms would also threaten the maintenance of barns that are currently in use, subjecting them to possible neglect and decay. The prospect of losing village farms threatens the identity of an active and authentic farming community.

My village was once common. The sad thing is that we have eroded and paved and sprawled so many other villages that my village has become unique. It worries me to think that this place may become a memory, or worse, "precious." Why is it when people move away from a place they want to escape, they end up bringing with them the very things they thought they were getting away from? More and more we find ourselves living in landscapes that are unrecognizable, undesirable, and inhospitable. We are all looking for a place worth living in; we are all looking for Eden. So why, then, do we end up creating empty landscapes that are just like the places we wanted to leave? ✍

For sale

Eleanor Garretson, high school student

In the past few years many houses have been built along my dirt road, and yet from my own windows I can see no other signs of human habitation except for the entrance of a neighbor's driveway and the road itself. Now a FOR SALE sign marks the property adjacent to ours and I wonder how much longer this area will remain so pure. Buried back into the forests on each side of the road there are houses, not immediately visible because their color and design match the landscape. With each new house I fear that the new people will maximize their own enjoyment of the landscape without respecting their fellow inhabitants or the well-being of the land.

When I was six, my family moved to Sheffield and into a new house designed by my father to look like it had been there for many years. Walking the boundaries of our property, I attempted to climb almost every tree and explored those that had fallen, scrambling over the torn roots. In the winter, I skated over the bumpy ice of Schenob Brook and in the summer, in search for flowers in the fen, my boots got stuck in concealed muddy holes. I pretended the rocks were my castles in the make-believe kingdom of my backyard.

As I grew attached to the land, my house also adapted. The dirty construction site became a grassy yard with trees and native bushes, such as sumac and witch hazel, comfortably scattered along the edge rather than rigidly confined into an artificial landscape formula. The outside color of the house weathered into a deep brown that echoed the tree trunks. As the gaudy newness faded from the house, branches extended over the back porch, conforming to its presence. Our chickens forage in our compost pile, hidden behind an old stone wall that curls through the trees directly behind the house. The proximity of the house to the forest allows even the south-facing terrace to always have some welcome shade. The forest approaches the house in a mass of textured greens present in the hemlocks, the swamp maples, the ash, and the white pines. Occasional glimpses of the adjoining grassy fen sneak through the overlapping branches. Through my kitchen window, I can observe deer ambling along the boundary of our yard or a pileated woodpecker noisily removing bugs from a dead tree. The animals seem oblivious to our human presence, and treat the yard as simply another natural clearing.

Along with my selfish wish to preserve the charm of my own property, I also unselfishly love and respect the Berkshires. I know that continual development is the reality of our county, yet human progress doesn't have to inevitably conflict with the needs of the environment. People who move here desire rural beauty, but I feel they often don't understand that this beauty springs from careful cooperation with the land. A house, even if it possesses an attractive design, is not truly magnificent unless it exists in harmony with its surroundings, blending to a more subtle and profound loveliness. ❧

To the Normanskill

David Yezzi, poet

The city blurs: our street a winding stream
we dig our heels in, not knowing it
the same way twice. The block of shops on 1st

transubstantiates itself each year,
as Peppermint Park clears for a doughnut shop,
or the something-we-forgot becomes a bank

or Chicken Fair, or just goes dark indefinitely.
Away, we feel we're freed from febrile change,
arriving upstate at a natural stream,

which, though it rises in the spring and dries
by midsummer, always returns (as we do).
Renewal resumes its human pace. This is

the place to bury something precious
that still will be here when, some decades on,
we come again with cares to dig it up.

And what will we uncover of these woods?
The stands of sumac and the wild irises
that flank the matted grass where deer have lain:

they come back the same. Also the same:
crab apples in the fall, and banks of silt
that intercut the woods with sinuous gray,

deposited like whales at the water's edge.
For miles, we've sunk-in something of ourselves,
left as a keepsake of our happiness.

And, if we aren't the ones to dig it up,
perhaps it will be found by those who follow us
onto this ground. And just as they were ours,
these memories will become their memories. ❧

Who lives with you?

Erik Kiviat, ecologist

I HAVE SEEN VERY LITTLE NEW CONSTRUCTION that responds sensitively to the ecology of a site. Too often subdivision lines disregard the natural contours, key features, or lay of the land. And thus begins a process of decision-making that is disconnected from the dynamics of ecology and wildlife habitats. Well-intentioned planners tend to focus on visual impacts and disregard the ecological content of the landscape. Putting a house in the woods to preserve the scenery of the fields, for example, may cause the least visual impact but not the least ecological impact. I am afraid that most planning and design processes are so human-centric that they fail to consider the important needs of wildlife. But building a house is an opportunity to protect and preserve nature and creatures as well as to create a perfect place to live.

Your first step towards ecological planning is to understand the special habitats of your property. Many species, including many of the less common biota to which we accord conservation value, have distinct affinities with particular habitats. If we lose these habitats, we endanger these species. In the Hudson Valley region, prickly-pear cactus usually grows near the Hudson River on sunny outcrops that are not too acidic. Several rare or vulnerable frogs and salamanders breed in intermittently flooded pools surrounded by forest. Bog turtles live in sunny, wet, limy meadows with soft soils and groundwater seepage. Slimy salamanders occupy shaded accumulations of rock fragments interspersed with soil beneath wooded slopes or ledges. And many other special habitats support special species. Unfortunately, the very habitats and land features that support rare native animals and plants too often become the places we disrupt through construction.

Not every landowner can be an expert field biologist but everyone can look for unusual features on the land. The unusual or unique-looking spots are probably just that, and

often support rare things, so should not be disturbed. Ridge tops, rock ledges and talus accumulations, groves or fringes of big trees, forests of unusual tree species composition, wetlands and their edges, streams and their flood plains, shores of natural lakes and ponds, caves, springs and seeps, sandy areas, and extensive grasslands or shrub lands are some of the types of habitats likely to support rare species. In general, more extensive patches of a particular habitat type, more extreme environmental conditions, and forests with more down wood, deeper leaf litter, and less compacted soil may be more valuable for biological diversity. Soil types of limited occurrence may support scarce habitats with rare species. Other things equal, land that has been less altered by construction, agriculture, or other human activities, and larger parcels, in more rural or wild settings, are more likely to support significant habitats in need of conservation.

Although many rare species are in the wilder or more natural environments, to some extent biodiversity is where you find it. I have found rare plants along railway lines, near busy highways or in the shale of an abandoned mine. If a species does not occur elsewhere in the region, or is declining greatly, then it may inhabit an altered environment. The important thing is to look carefully and obtain an assessment from a qualified biologist, botanist or wildlife specialist.

Knowing who lives on your land before you decide where you build may save you trouble. I know new homeowners who were surprised to find that they shared their south-facing slope in the Catskills with rattlesnakes. The rattlesnakes like to sun themselves at the foot of their wall where the house and parking area concentrate solar heat. This is also true in a subdivision at the base of the Taconic Mountains where rattlesnakes seeking water concentrate at an abandoned quarry pond during droughts. Being a distance from a mosquito-breeding habitat or outside the potential

flooding zone of an active beaver dam are other ways to make our homes more livable while limiting our impact on species that play important roles in our ecological system.

Consider these fundamental measures as you evaluate your potential ecological impact. Make use of an existing driveway, well, septic system, storage shed, garden, structure, or other element of your domestic landscape so that you will not create new disturbances. If you site your home close to an existing road, you are likely to reduce disturbance to habitat interiors and obviate the need for long driveways that fragment habitat. Although hiding homes in the forest edge may preserve scenic open space, it can greatly affect the quality of the forest habitat for animals that require large tracts of unbroken forest. These animals may be disturbed by your noise and light, risk crossing driveways, or suffer from the loss of specific resources such as a spring, rock outcrop, or large tree.

By assessing the biological resources of your site, you may protect and conserve a valuable habitat or species as well as create a special natural place you can enjoy. If you own land on the west side of the Hudson River, you can take pride in not building on the ledge with the rock cresses eaten by the caterpillars of the falcate orange-tip butterfly, or in a woodland pool where wood frogs and marbled salamanders breed. If you own land in the Harlem Valley, you can enjoy not clearing the marble knoll with its limy sand soil for the gazebo and rock garden.

Instead look for nature's existing rock garden, lichen community, garden pool, jewel-like dragonfly, view, flowering shrub, and delicate grass flowers glinting in the sun. You might even buy land and not build on it at all! ❧

Cathedrals, barns & ponds

Allan Shope, architect

I HAVE BEEN AN ARCHITECT FOR TWENTY YEARS, designing houses for smart and interesting people. Most of my clients begin the architectural process thinking about what size house they want, what style the house should be, an appropriate cost, a time schedule for construction and what materials they will need. While these are all worthwhile considerations, they don't necessarily create good architecture, which is why I try to redirect the focus of everyone's attention to issues that are at the heart of meaningful design.

I developed my understanding of architecture during simple boyhood experiences in Connecticut. Our community grew shade tobacco for making cigar wrappers which is grown under nets to protect it from hail stones. It is then dried in barns to remove enough moisture from the leaves so that it can be shipped without mildewing. Tobacco barns are simple utilitarian buildings, two hundred feet long by forty-four feet wide. Architects did not design them and beauty was not a factor in planning them. Most of these barns are positioned on a north to south axis with the morning sun entering broadside. Early each morning during August the barns need to be opened for tractor access and ventilation. A tobacco barn is opened by unlatching the large doors on their ends and folding them back onto the corner of the barn. The interior of the barn is dark and cool from the night and a little scary. You step into the darkness, take seven paces to the right, fumble around for a latch, lift it and fold a hinged board on the side of the barn into the open position.

At once you feel a sense of relief as the morning sun slices across the darkness. This is repeated eighty-eight times as you work your way down to the other end of the barns, as darkness gives way to a pattern of light and shadow alternating on the dirt floor. At the far end, you fasten the wide door hasps so that the tractor can exit. Once the end doors are secured, you work your way back to where you began by opening every other one of the sideboards on the untouched length of the barn. When your work is completed, you are standing in the same location where you began twenty minutes earlier, looking at an entirely different architecture.

What had been darkness is now an aisle defined by wood columns converging in the distance in a beautiful display of perspective. Your eye races down the aisle, dancing over the rhythm of light and shadow created by the morning sun. Simple contrasts become profound. The enclosure of the barn is comforting because of the vastness of the fields beyond. The stillness of the barn structure contrasts with the movement of the sun-heated steam rising out of the dirt floor. The man-made structure of the barn stands out against the soft natural forms around it. Together these contrasts build a powerful and emotional experience.

Ten years after I became familiar with the aesthetic attributes of a tobacco barn I went to Europe for the first time and visited a gothic cathedral. I joined a guided tour of Chartre, a building that had taken 400 years to build. No expenses had been spared. Saints had been buried in its floor, over six million pieces of colored glass had been soldered together to form its stained glass windows, and by all accounts it is one of the great architectural achievements of western civilization. I listened intently to our guide discuss the gargoyles and the flying buttresses and the history of the building. Each visitor's excitement was palpable. None of my amazement seemed related to the gargoyles or the dead saints or the flying buttresses. I felt like I was back in the tobacco barn. The enormous stone columns along the main aisle of the church converged to create the perspective of the barn's aisle; the movement of the smoke from the memorial candles contrasted with the stillness of the stone church and reminded me of the steam rising from the dirt floor of the barn; the rhythm of light and shadow created by the clerestory of the church echoed the pattern of morning light entering the barn through the ventilation slats; the view down the main aisle of the great cathedral out to the village square evoked the same response as the view from the barn out to the fields. Each building offered a sense of comfort and enclosure from within made more powerful by the vastness and mystery of what lay beyond it. Stylistically, functionally, and historically these buildings had nothing in common with each another and yet they evoked similar emotions.

When clients ask for a Tudor house or a French chateau, I challenge them to search beyond style or magazine photographs in order to define the essential qualities of a building that will more truly inspire and please them. We may visit a structure, like the tobacco barn, or a place on their land to understand how qualities of light or rhythm or forms affect them. Together we examine the distinctions of their land—its topography, lines of hedgerows and stonewalls, or changing lights in hope that this experience will transcend their presumptions about style, material and size.

I was with a couple recently who upon purchasing their land wanted to immediately make improvements. They intended to clean their forest, dredge their pond, and fertilize their fields. As a way of challenging their assumptions, I requested a pre-dawn meeting at their land. As the darkness gave way to light, a crescendo of sounds graced the valley. Delicate songbirds pierced the air as skilled woodwinds. Turkeys boomed, ruffed grouse drummed, frogs burped like bassoons, water spiders danced, and kingfishers swooped over the pond like the coordinating hands of a great conductor. It was in every respect an inspiring harmonic symphony. As we headed back to the car, the symphony was silenced in fear, and it was apparent that my clients had learned two simple things. The first was that if they proceeded with their precon-ceptions, the symphony would be gone and only a shallow song would be left. The second was that they they wanted their house to make a statement about protecting the symphony and becoming a part of it rather than dominating it. Not a word had been spoken. They started to imagine how their land itself would be a source of inspiration for the making of a distinct and fitting house. ❧

No UFO

Chris Garrity, realtor

THE ERA OF BUILDING large sprawling homes is over. My customers are looking for high quality and detailed finishes and they see through fluff. When one couple sought my advice about building their retirement home to replace their seasonal weekend cabin, I asked them why they loved their cabin so much. Their reasons included the rustic character, the intimate size and the way it was tucked low along the pond. In the end, they built a modest sized and high quality home. When you drive up their driveway, it appears as if their cabin has simply been enlarged and that their house has been there since the 1920s.

On the other hand, a former customer who bought a thirty-acre plot of land sited their house on an open north facing hilltop where the wind blew hard and cold. Facing north cost them in the long run. And it was not something their thermostat could fix; air is like water, it reaches what it seeks. Their brand new $50,000 wood shingle roof needed continual shingle replacement. With the strong winds, the rain moved sideways, sneaking up and under their shingles. Their steep parcel of land eroded before they installed a costly landscaping plan. The slow percolation rates of their soil type increased the cost of their septic system. I am not preaching that they should not have chosen the top of the ridge, since I sold them this property with the view as its primary value. I simply hoped they would consider the impact of their site on both their life and their community. Even if they could afford the oil bills and the construction costs, there are ethical impacts to being in broad view.

The view is an important value element, but how you create the home in relation to the land can either enhance or diminish the view. Build a Gwathmey contemporary, period saltbox or a converted barn, but build it where it works with the land. Style is a personal choice. I only urge that you strive to fit your house with the surrounding environs. Although I don't care for what I call the "vicontemponial shingle" home, a mish-mash of styles including Victorian, Contemporary and Colonial sheathed in wood shingles to give it that country flair, any style can work if it works with the property. In Kent, Connecticut there is an incredibly beautiful contemporary home with an all-glass wall facing a large waterfall. Another of my favorites, built within the last ten years, is a stone house that seems to grow out of the rock it is placed upon. Yet, too often this sensitivity is missing, made more apparent by the over-sized house.

I heard of a woman riding on the local hunt who reared her horse upon entering a lovely field and seeing a house on a distant ridge. She remarked to her friend how insensitive the owner was to paint a house such a brilliant white that could be seen for miles. He agreed and informed her it was her house. She later had her house painted in a more subdued tone. Sunlight reflecting off bright paint and windows and outdoor lighting can be incredibly intrusive for miles. There is a house in Kent, Connecticut that is dubbed "the UFO house." As darkness masks the precipice that the house sits so heavily upon, the landscape lighting creates a scene from the *X Files*.

Before you build your dream house, I recommend that you experience your land in all types of weather and through all seasons. View your site from miles away and from your immediate neighborhood. Endeavor to understand how your land had been used before you bought it. Get to know your property before you decide where you want to settle your home. Without this knowledge, how else will you come to know your land, your responsibility to it and the type of home that will really fulfill your dreams? ❧

A bend in the road

Laura Hammond Toonkel, artist

ALTHOUGH WE DO NOT YET KNOW ONE ANOTHER we have something in common. We both share an affinity with the beautiful land that surrounds us. I have lived with this land for many years and feel its many connections. This land has linked five generations of my family. For three it provided sustenance by the daily sweat, frustration, and joy of our small working farm. Today it provides a different kind of sustenance. Although my children may never work this land and harvest its yield, the land sustains and nurtures them with its intrinsic natural beauty. As a child I was taught to respect my environment, not taking from it what I did not need. I have encouraged my children to carry the same respect for their surroundings.

Every day when I walk the rugged hills and fallow fields that surround my home I am grateful to have the opportunity to enjoy open space. I appreciate being able to look across expanses of undulating fields punctuated with groves of deciduous woodland and to see just that—the graceful rhythms of the land unblemished by the encroachment of human activity. I am thankful to have neighbors who value undeveloped tracts of land and who understand that our human presence does not have to overwhelm the landscape. Because of the vision and sensitivity of others, I have the opportunity to enjoy vistas near and far that are part of an interconnected natural system. I do not take these opportunities for granted, because they are quickly vanishing. Without thoughtful consideration of the impact of increased development, the vulnerable balance of these environmental elements may be altered, prohibiting this land to sustain us with its beauty and vital resources.

As an artist my creative spirit is inspired and nourished by the rhythms and pulse of this land. I have developed a series of works that investigates changing compositional qualities of this landscape, both visually and ecologically.

For one series, I focused upon a small wetland beside a dirt road. This small stretch of road reminds me that my ancestors once depended upon this route to get their milk to market. Today it offers a different kind of survival. As I enter its arched portal of canopied trees, I am transported to a place of quiet refuge. Perhaps it is the contrast of the flooded light compared to the dense canopy of wooded growth, the interesting salamanders and newts that migrate across the road, the abundance of life that blooms each spring from the rich organic decay of the past season, or the visually complex layers of disintegrating vegetation that hold my fascination. As I paint and draw this small wetland patch, it teaches me a great deal. I witness the dramatic seasonal and daily changes that occur in a small place. I learn about the importance of wetland habitats regardless of their size. I reaffirm a desire that has become a constant theme in my work of celebrating the ordinary. It is easy to overlook an intimate scene like this bend in the road. A small pool of water, a fallen decayed tree, and dead leaves challenge traditional ideas about what is beautiful and what is worth painting. But by looking through its changing layers and watching its constant evolution, this ordinary place becomes surprisingly extraordinary.

As a landowner, the excitement and enthusiasm you have for developing the vision of your property may compare to my experience of beginning a new painting. We both face the challenge of integrating our perceptions and sensibilities with an existing environment. I try to honestly interpret the landscape in inspiring ways. I am not interested in idealizing the relationship of the forms that I see. In my compositions I do not edit entire groups of trees or eliminate hillsides for the sake of a balanced composition. I begin my process of working by covering my blank canvas with a layer of saturated color. This base penetrates the fibers of my surface and provides a support for other layers to be built upon, similar to the layers of rich organic muck that support an explosion of life in the vernal pool. Although I do not physically labor with the soil as my ancestors did, I feel a strong tactile interaction with the earth as I express the nuances of forms that inspire me through the strokes of my brush. As my image evolves I am often surprised by unexpected relationships of color, surface textures, and perceptions of depth. Having a creative dialog with these organic developments gives my work expressive potential and prevents it from following pre-determined notions. Perhaps as your work develops and the layers reveal themselves, you will discover unexpected ideas based upon the unique qualities of your land.

As this region faces the pressures of increased development, the open vistas, the rural character, and the bucolic beauty that attract so many newcomers to this area today may be gone tomorrow. It is my hope that new landowners and long-time residents will work individually and cooperatively toward a balance that recognizes the inevitable growth but acknowledges how we need to sensitively consider the land's qualities as we grow. It is my hope we can work together to preserve the openness of the landscape and protect the natural resources that we share and depend upon. I hope we can see ourselves as stewards of this land whose collective efforts will leave a legacy that sustains the children of future generations. ❧

Spring visitors

Fernando Nottebohm, biologist

IT IS AN OVERCAST DAY, late in March; the snow has melted and the ground has begun to thaw. As I walk away from my house, in the dim twilight of evening, I hear the unmistakable sound, "peent," pause, "peent," delivered in a monotonous, penetrating manner. The biologist in me is aroused, for this is the sound of the woodcock and it is the first one I have heard this year. The woodcocks are back!

Woodcocks are in the same family as sandpipers, but unlike their typically coastal cousins, woodcocks are common inland birds. Woodcocks depend on humid, loamy soils rich in worms, their staple, which they find by probing the ground with their long bill. They have enormous eyes, set back on their head, perhaps to watch for predators while their bill explores for food. My special fondness for woodcocks has to do with their arrival in early spring, when much of the countryside still has the drab colors of winter. I do not see them arrive, but I hear them once they are back.

After the male has produced a string of five to ten "peents," it rockets into the air and as it climbs in a wide spiral produces an ever faster and shriller twittering sound. This ascent ends suddenly. As the bird zigzags back to earth it breaks into rushed, melodious chipping notes that so fill the air that they seem to come from all directions. Each flight ends at exactly the same spot where it commenced, and it is to that spot that a willing female must come to find her mate. This display, which starts about half an hour after sundown, continues until it gets full dark. It occurs once more in the twilight of dawn. If you focus your binoculars on the general area from which the "peenting" comes and stand looking towards the lighter part of the sky, you will see the silhouette of the woodcock taking to the air, its ascent and then its erratic twists and turns as it returns to ground. It is a display pregnant with the promises of spring and one of its earliest harbingers. If your land includes moist alder thickets, spring-fed hillside runs or rich, moist bottom lands, you are quite likely to receive, every spring, the visit of these early neighbors. If you leave those parts of your land alone (late mowing of fields will not disturb breeding), you will have woodcocks back every year and with them, their unique, virtuoso aerial performance.

That takes care of one of the earliest arrivals. Now, for a late one, the bobolink. The bobolink, a songbird, returns for the breeding season as late as early May, more than a month after the woodcock. This is a grassland bird common in the Midwest. Its presence in New England owes much to a habitat that in this part of the country is usually man-made. Bobolinks are a bit smaller than a robin and the female, which is drab brown, is likely to go unnoticed. Not so the male, who has a black face and neck, a bright yellow nape and a white rump and wing bar. I learn of the bobolinks' arrival because one morning there will be several perched on the tall grass heads in the field by my house. They sing their bubbling song from these vantage points. Periodically they rise into the air and carry their song higher. They also sing as they flutter over their territory with a slow, butterfly-like cadence. Sometimes two males will fly and sing in this manner side by side along a shared territorial boundary. Bobolinks continue to sing until late June, when breeding ends. Bobolinks winter in the grasslands of South America.

The secret to entice these late visitors is to mow the fields late, not before mid July. If this is done, bobolinks will be back year after year to regale you with their aerial and vocal displays. Late mowing will not affect the quality of your grassland. There is still plenty of time for Queen Anne's Lace to push through the stubble and grow the lovely blossoms that later, dry, will rise above the snow. However, late mowing may jeopardize the blossoming of milkweed, so if your field has bobolinks during the summer, it may not have monarch

butterflies in the fall. The caterpillar of monarch butterflies feeds on the foliage of milkweeds. If you also want to encourage these lovely butterflies which, by the way, are long-range migrants that winter in Mexico, you may do so by leaving unmowed a patch in the field where milkweeds grow best.

Thus, small adjustments in the way you manage your land will determine who visits, who stays, who breeds and, most importantly, who will be back next year. This can be a source of great satisfaction and pride to the rural landowner that listens to the voices of the land. You will know, too, that your land is a good place to live, not just for you, but also for many others. ❧

A place in mind

Peter Forbes, writer and farmer

THERE IS A MYSTERY in how we have come to know this place that is not unlike the mystery of falling in love with someone. Eighteen months ago, we barely knew the boundaries of our farm or the source of our affections for it. We spent those first months putting our feet on its trails and our fingers in its soils, confident of its beauty and naive about its quality. Then there have been times when being here has felt entirely overwhelming, when we worried about our abilities and lost our sense of purpose, or when the land has felt uncomfortable, like clothes that don't yet fit. We have been slowly growing into this land.

We agonized over where to cut hay, and then reveled in the greenness of the fields and the satisfaction of stacking the bales in our barn. We watched the springs dry up and came to know angst as a weather system. We are still frightened by the wind—so fierce on this hillside—but have learned to lean into it in the day and to be held by it at night. We have studied the grass and moved our sheep through the pastures and thus come to know the pleasure of their nourishment. We have camped on the hilltop through heavy rains and slept with the story that this mountain has felt a million such storms. We've crossed these fields with our soaked legs to watch the sun rise over a valley buried in fog. We've fed others and ourselves from this land, and now carry it in us wherever we go. Today, my eye is drawn to a familiar view of where the fields meet the sky and I wonder what it will be like to look upon this land when we are old and bent over. What started by chance has been now graced by intention. This land has become a marriage, but no less a mystery.

We came to this hillside in search of a more satisfying bond with the world around us: one about community, not isolation. We came here out of the growing recognition of what might nourish our family most. We came here to engage and to serve differently, and we sense that knowing this place well leads us to where, in our best selves, we really want to go.

We want to trust and be trusted. We want to be firmly rooted here, independent and self-willed, with a sense of security that is as deep as the list of people we can call when things go wrong. We all have relationships and some aren't good ones. We enter into these with the aspiration of being at our very best, but the truth is that we aren't always perfect. Often I fail. My relationship to this hillside is transforming me. It is teaching me how to pay closer attention, to go beyond what I see on the surface, to be more patient. I am slowly cultivating myself by attending to the particulars of the soil, the flow of water, the diversity of life, and the burden this land and we can carry. This land is filled with both seeds and ashes, and my struggle to understand both has made for a more mature love. Our relationship to this farm is about health and well-being: the land's, our neighbors', and ours.

Understanding this hillside has helped me to see what is sacred and essential in myself and in others. What has grown most for me this year, what results from any healthy relationship, is my own emotional intelligence. I see that all we need is already at hand. Through this place, what matters most becomes apparent. It is this: In every living thing there is the longing for love and the desire to be healthy with the rest of living things.

One late afternoon I walk across our high pasture when I see a bit of movement along the fence line. Then she emerges from the shadows, a black bear who walks purposefully out into the tall grass and across to a cherry tree. Her size and wildness takes my breath away. I watch from above until she smells me and retreats, leaving on the barbed wire a tangle of her fur that I now carry in a pouch. Her fur merges there with the wool of our Icelandic sheep until I can no longer tell them apart. I carry the pouch to remind me of all the sets of relationships, including my own, that are this land. Each day my love of this place becomes wildness inside of me, a reminder of my attachments to this world. ❧

About our contributors

Executive Editor

Stephen Kaye is a retired attorney, a farmer and former member of the board of the Dutchess Land Conservancy. He raises beef cows in the Hudson Valley where he started a cooperative for other grass-fed-beef farmers.

Editor

Jamie Crelly Purinton co-authored *Landscape Narratives: Design Practices for Telling Stories* with Matthew Potteiger. She lives in the Hudson Valley where she practices landscape architecture.

Photographer

Charles Lindsay's first books, *Mentawai Shaman: Keeper of the Rain Forest* and *Turtle Islands: Balinese Ritual and the Green Turtle,* portray Indonesian cultures and their relationships to nature. For his latest book, *Upstream: Fly Fishing in the American West,* Lindsay brings us into the rivers of the American West. Although his work takes him around the world, he calls Rensselaerville, New York home.

Book Designer

Rich Kraham designs books, visual identities, and environmental graphics from his main street office in downtown Chatham, New York.

Writers (in order of appearance)

Michael Pollan is the author of *Second Nature: A Gardener's Education, A Place of My Own: The Education of an Amateur Builder,* and most recently *The Botany of Desire: A Plant's-Eye View of the World.* He is currently writing a book about the food chain and teaching journalism at Berkeley. He lives on an old dairy farm in Cornwall Bridge, Connecticut.

Le Anne Schreiber is an independent journalist and writer of essays, memoirs and criticism. At present she is working on a book about the life she made and found on Snyder Pond in Copake, New York.

Don MacLean and his wife Marnie grow organic fruits and vegetables on the Thompson-Finch Farm in Ancram, New York. Don also chairs the local planning board.

Bill Bensen is chef and owner of The Palmer House Cafe located in the hamlet of Rensselaerville, New York. His gourmet restaurant is a community gathering place that features locally produced ingredients.

Jennifer Brady-Connor is a wetland specialist working for the Land Trust Alliance in Saratoga Springs, New York.

Robbie Butler is a silversmith and avid mushroom collector in Pine Plains, N.Y.

Charles Canham is a forest ecologist working at the Institute of Ecosystem Studies in Millbrook, New York. He studies the ways that humans shape forested landscapes around the world.

Barry Chase and his wife Rosie take care of 125 Holsteins on a farm formerly owned by his father. Their family farm is one of the few remaining small dairy farms in Dutchess County, New York.

Jens Braun is working with family and friends in Canaan, New York to create a new Quaker community that will fit the ecology of their 135-acre property.

Barbara A. Hermance is a realtor and land consultant living in Colum-bia County, New York. For the last fifteen years, she chaired the Taghkanic Zoning Board.

Linda Anderson lives in Cambridge, New York where she's active in local planning issues. She has worked as a reporter for both National Public Radio and *The New York Times*.

Eleanor Garretson is a student at Carleton College. She grew up in Sheffield, Massachusetts.

David Yezzi is the author of *The Hidden Model: Poems and Sad Is Eros*. He is an associate editor of *Parnassus: Poetry in Review* and director of the Unterberg Poetry Center of the 92nd Street Y in New York City.

Erik Kiviat is an ecologist and co-founder of Hudsonia, a not-for-profit environmental institute for the Hudson Valley. Erik recently co-wrote a Biodiversity Assessment Manual for the Hudson River Estuary Corridor with Hudsonia.

Allan Shope is an architect and founder of the Listening Rock Farm and Environmental Center in Amenia, New York.

Chris Garrity owns a real estate firm in Kent and Sharon, Connecticut. He is involved in local efforts to balance land conservation with sensitive site development.

Laura Hammond Toonkel has spent most of her life living on her family's farm in the Hudson Valley where she works as an artist and raises a family.

Fernando Nottebohm is a biologist working at the Rockefeller Institute. His special area of research is the vocal behavior of birds.

Peter Forbes is the editor of *Our Land, Ourselves: Reading on People and Place,* and the author of *The Great Remembering*. He farms with his family in the Mad River Valley of Vermont.

PLATES

Cover: *Fisher, Southwest Albany County*
     1 *Shagbark hickory leaf buds*
     2 *Common barn-owl*
     3 *Sedges and rushes, calcareous fen*
     4 *Calcareous fen*
     5 *American toad, Charlie's pond*
     6 *Holstein cow, Chase Farm*
     7 *Ramp flower stalks, July*
     8 *Polypody ferns*
     9 *Cattail*
    10 *Pond lilies*
    11 *Hen of the woods*
    12 *Cap mushroom*
    13 *Black locust grove*
    14 *Chase's Holstein cows*
    15 *Fisher*
    16 *Paper birch*
    17 *Hemlock grove*
    18 *Short-eared owl*
    19 *Iris, Charlie's Pond*
    20 *Round hay bale*
    21 *Corn tassels*
    22 *Woodland*
    23 *Spring runoff*
    24 *Fisher*
    25 *Jack-in-the-pulpit*
    26 *Eastern red cedars*
    27 *Cattails*
    28 *Screech owls*
    29 *Birch catkins in spring snow*
    30 *Blooming hawthorn*
    31 *Red-wing blackbirds*
    32 *Red-tailed hawk*
    33 *Windrow*
    34 *Ten Mile Creek*
    35 *Black Dome*
    36 *Thompson-Finch Farm*
    37 *Porcupines*

PHOTOGRAPHER'S NOTE:

Voices of the Land was commissioned by the Dutchess Land Conservancy and a community of people who were questioning what was happening to the land around them. These photographs are from two years of periodic wandering through forests, fields, and wetlands to observe and photograph on behalf of this community. I returned to my favorite locations throughout the seasons to witness their change—to reflect and work in different light. Moving slowly through a landscape I'm drawn in visually, but also by the smells and sounds: locust trees flowering, toads, and screech owls calling in the fog, wind cracking the branches, and the smell of mint trampled by deer down by my pond. These are photographs from the extended place that I call home. ❧

All photographs appearing in *Voices of the Land* were made with a twin lens *Rolleiflex*. Limited edition photographs from *Voices of the Land* are available by contacting Gitterman Gallery, 170 East 75th Street, New York, New York 10021 212.734.0868, www.gittermangallery.com. Further information about Charles Lindsay is available by visiting his website www.charleslindsey.com

Please contact Chelsea Green about the traveling exhibition for *Voices of the Land*.

Acknowledgments

Voices of the Land started with conversations between Stephen Kaye and his neighbors. Although the discussion began as a reaction to the sight of large new houses being built on old farm fields and hilltops, it grew in content and gained the depth of a wide community. The negative reactions evolved into strong affirmatins on the value and importance of our shared landscape. I want to thank Stephen Kaye for supporting this book from the beginning and letting it take its own form to the finish.

We would like to acknowledge the support of Peter Tcherepnine for underwriting a good portion of the book, and to our friends and colleagues Wendy Curtis, John Dyson, Woody Keesee and Terry Regan who provided important and timely support. The Dutchess Land Conservancy provided valuable assistance in backing *Voices of the Land*.

We thank all the contributing writers who took time away from their busy lives to put their thoughts and experiences into words. We are all the more grateful for their efforts since many of them felt unaccustomed to writing. We would also like to thank Jennifer Groff, Tad Higgins and Darcy Purinton for providing creative input and thoughtful reviews.

We thank Kelly Martin in Rensselaerville for help with the animals and owls, Jonathan Wood and The Raptor Project, Victor Schrager for introductions to those wildlife rehabilitators, Bill Bensen and The Palmer House Cafe in Rensselaerville, Sergio Purtell at Black and White on White photo lab in New York City, and all the people who gladly let Charlie Lindsay wander around their lands for photographs.

We immediately felt confident in the experienced hands of Chelsea Green Publishing Company. Margo Baldwin, publisher, knew how to fulfill our book's philosophy and intentions. As managing editor, Collette Fugere eagle-eyed the manuscript and moved the book efficiently through the publishing process; and Peter Holm, production manager, carefully insured the book's final quality.

Our gratitude to all of our supporters may be best expressed by inspiring you to take better care of our landscape. Together we have the power to create a community land ethic that honors, respects, and protects all the life that shares this land. ❧

Designed by Rich Kraham

Printed in Canada by Friesens on Jenson Matte, a recycled paper with
10% post-consumer waste content

First printing, January 2004

10 9 8 7 6 5 4 3 2 1

Library of Congress Cataloging-in-Publication Data

Voices of the land / edited by Jamie Crelly Purinton ; photographs by
Charles Lindsay ; foreword by Michael Pollan.
      p. cm.
ISBN 1-931498-50-4
1. Nature. 2. Land use. I. Purinton, Jamie.
QH81.V85 2004
333.73'16 — dc22

                                   2003026611

Chelsea Green Publishing Company
Post Office Box 428
White River Junction, VT 05001
(800) 639-4099
www.chelseagreen.com